THE Homeless Hotdogs

How Jesus changed the face of downtown Oklahoma City

a memoir

Aaron Stimpson

STIMPSON PUBLISHING

Contents

ABOUT THE AUTHOR

Aaron Stimpson was born in Amarillo, Texas. He has lived in various states, especially Oklahoma, which serves as the backdrop of this book. A devoted follower of Jesus, he is passionate about nurturing the church and empowering others through spiritual education.

Happily married to Sarah, they have engaged in transformative missionary work in India, deepening their faith and connecting with diverse cultures. Their love for travel fosters relationships with Christians around the globe.

Now residing in South Carolina, he inspires others with his insights and commitment to spiritual growth, making a meaningful impact in his community.

"Come and you will see." John 1:39

"Follow me." John 1:43

Again Jesus spoke to them, saying, "I am the light of the world. Whoever follows me will not walk in darkness, but will have the light of life." John 8:12

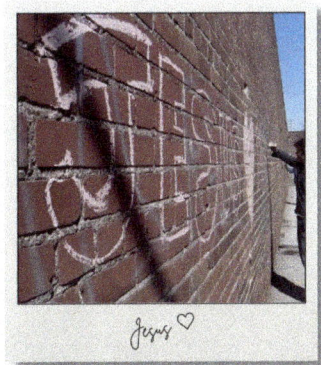

Jesus ♡

INVITATION

Dear fellow seeker,

As you turn these pages, I hope you discover echoes of your story woven into ours.

Although you may find parallels of Scripture illustrated by the testimonies of God within these texts, you will not find a Bible study or a devotional book. Instead, this is a Masterclass in how Jesus called a multitude of people to Himself as he orchestrated something extraordinary in downtown Oklahoma City. You will witness stories from the vantage point of those people.

Fair warning: some parts may seem, at first glance, to be offensive, but that's not the intention. We lay our hearts bare within these memories, sharing our raw and unvarnished experiences.

If you choose to stick around, and I sincerely hope you do, I'd love to hear about your experiences with the love of Jesus. The good, the bad, and the sometimes painful.

My hope is that you are deeply inspired and motivated to seek Jesus and His Holy Spirit's guidance and sincerely ask Him where He is at work and how you can participate in His plans for your community.

Between the bustling streets and towering sky-scrapers of Oklahoma City, something unusual was making its way through downtown. It wasn't marked with the usual fanfare, grand announce-ments, or spectacles found in many ministries. Instead, it was a quiet, irresistible revolution of God's people being called back to Him through His glorious acts of faith and grace.

This story is about ordinary people experiencing the extraordinary - a time when worship songs like God of this City by Chris Tomlin, Revela-tion Song by Gateway Worship, God of Wonders by Paul Baloche, and Lead Me to the Cross by Hillsong UNITED, to name a few, were there to inspire us.

God orchestrates the seemingly mundane into something magnificent, weaving individual sto-ries into His grand narrative.

DISCLAIMER: Alright, here we go—disclaimer time! Now, I'm not exactly jumping for joy at the thought of writing one of these, but here we are. So, let's get this straight: this book is definitely not a manifesto for a rogue ministry or advocation of such. We embarked on this journey because we felt a divine nudge from God and we did so under the watchful eye and loving guidance of our church leader during that season. I'm all in for accountability and love when it comes to the church. After all, the church is God's trusty vehicle for spreading good news to the world. Embrace the love and accountability as we navigate this adventure together.

AS YOU READ

I'll start by telling the bad news first.

Don't worry.

It's short, but then we will get to the good news!

THE BAD BIT

Chapter One

THROUGH DIVINE FRUSTRATION

As Sarah and I attended various churches, we often found ourselves caught between the allure of modern worship experiences and our desire for deeper spiritual nourishment. The bustling atmosphere, complete with coffee bars, state-of-the-art sound systems, large crowds, and popcorn, created an undeniable energy. Yet, we couldn't shake the feeling that something essential was missing.

Imagine the scene from "Gladiator." You know the one - where Russell Crowe's character, surrounded by a cathedral of bloodthirsty spectators, defiantly shouts, "Are you not entertained?!"

We were certainly entertained. The worship teams and teachers put on a show that would make Cirque du Soleil jealous, with a few Bible verses sprinkled in for good measure. This, we were told, was "getting people saved."

Sarah and I were baffled. I'd flip through the Bible at home, squinting at the pages as if the words might rearrange themselves to match what we were experiencing every Sunday. They never did.

We would try throwing ourselves wholeheartedly into church life, joining home groups, and volunteering at every opportunity. We hoped to forge meaningful connections and find ways to grow in our faith. We encountered well-intentioned programs that lacked direction and outreach initiatives that fell short of their potential. These experiences left us wondering about the true nature of discipleship and service in what was sold as the progressive, updated modern church.

Despite moments of discouragement, we felt compelled to continue seeking a church that would focus on the life of Jesus, full of the Holy Spirit, having vibrant worship with well-rooted teaching and active service to the surrounding community. We believed such a gathering of believers must exist – one that embraced the full spectrum of faith in what the Scriptures in the Lord's Prayer, a desire to have "Your Kingdom come, On Earth as it is in Heaven."

As we continued our journey, we realized we weren't alone in our search. We met countless others who shared our hunger. Some had grown disillusioned, retreating to ill-advised solitary spiritual practices, while others persevered in their search for a community that resonated with their opinions and view of the world.

Just when we thought we might have to compromise, an unexpected yet well-timed encounter changed everything.

THE GOOD BIT

SPRING

Chapter Two

JESUS GATHERING HIS PEOPLE

WE DISCOVERED THAT GOD was orchestrating a beautiful symphony across the city. His divine hand was touching the hearts of others, drawing them into a grand design that was only beginning to unfold.

Encountering kindred spirits like Tim & Leanne, whose passion for community service, ministry, and vision was instrumental in catalyzing critical decision-makers in the city. Ryan E, whose boldness is legendary; Ben, who brought the challenge; Jose and Samantha, who carried their expertise in ministering to individuals less fortunate with their unrelenting faith in Jesus, while Kim's gift for being able to resource others came in immensely handy. Caesar's heart to reach the lost added a new dimension to our gatherings. Ryan K's leadership and ability to gather people helped grow a healthy community. Mark & Marsha's leadership skills helped shape our growing community through prayer and acts of kindness. Crystal and Jason's dedication complemented the whole community that Jesus was beginning to build. Andrew and Sylvia, being hot off the mission field, led the way in ministry and generosity.

Countless others, including ourselves, found their place in this tapestry of faith and purpose. Each person's journey downtown is a testament to God's intricate workings, their stories intertwining to create a powerful narrative of divine guidance.

As this diverse group of individuals came together, we witnessed the formation of a living, breathing illustration of God's church in action. It was as if the body of Christ was assembling before our eyes, each member vital and purposeful. This convergence of souls, all called to this specific time and place, painted a breathtaking picture of how God moves among His people, nurturing and guiding His Bride, the Church, towards a greater purpose.

What follows is a snapshot of what God did as we stood in awe of His perfect timing and intricate planning, realizing that we were part of something far more significant than ourselves – a movement of faith, hope, and love blossoming in the heart of our city.

Chapter Three

OLD DEFUNCT GROCERY STORE

EACH PERSON HAS A story of how God eventually drew them downtown. Sarah recalls the beginning of our story,

> "As I was wiping down the espresso machine, lost in thought about our seemingly endless search for a meaningful church community when it caught the eye of fellow barista Ben. Maybe it was how I sighed or the far-away look in my eyes, but something prompted Ben to ask, 'Rough day!?' Before I knew it, I was pouring out the frustrations like a perfectly pulled shot of espresso - rich, intense, and a lit-

tle bitter. Ben listened, nodding along, his eyes growing wider with each detail. As I finished, he leaned in, a conspiratorial glint in his eye. 'You should come to my church,' barely containing his excitement. Aaron and I had heard that line before. More times than we could count.

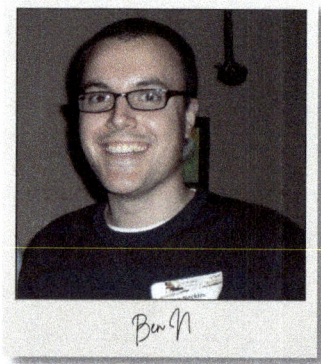

Ben N

However, something about Ben's invitation was different. Maybe it was how he said it, or we were desperate enough to try anything. Either way, we thought, 'How bad could it be?' After all, here was a fellow coffee slinger who actually seemed to enjoy going to church. We were grasping at straws, but at least this one came with a shot of espresso. That weekend, we stood in front of what looked like an abandoned grocery store. The faded sign above the door and the empty parking lot didn't exactly scream 'House of God.' It was more 'House of Forgotten Produce.' But something - curiosity, desperation, or maybe just the lingering effects of too much caffeine - made us push open that worn-out door."

Inside, it was like stepping into a bizarre time capsule. Empty shelves lined the walls, ghostly reminders of aisles once filled with canned goods and cereal boxes. But in one corner, someone had laid out a large rug, surrounded by a mishmash of chairs that looked like they'd been rescued from a yard sale and old café booths that had seen better days. You could almost see the phantom trails left by shopping carts long gone. Two tall floor lamps cast a warm glow over the space.

Kamps store

As we settled into our seats - mine creaked a little - Ben stepped to the front. Yes, that Ben, barista Ben. Turns out he wasn't just a church-goer; he was the pastor. Talk about failing to mention one of the most essential details.

He opened his mouth, and I no-lie, the words that came out nearly sent us sprinting for the exit: "If you came here looking for a church, I'm sorry, but this is not church."

Sarah and I exchanged panicked glances. Had we accidentally stumbled into some kind of coffee-fueled cult or one of those "Anonymous" groups?

But before we could make a break for it, Ben continued, "Church is what happens out there, in the community, in how we love and serve others and gather together." I had never heard of such a thing. Was this guy out of his mind, or was he trying to get us to see through a different lens?

It was like someone had flipped a switch in my brain. All those years of searching for the "perfect" Sunday service, the right program, the ideal small group—this guy in skinny jeans and a T-shirt told us we'd been looking in all the "wrong places."

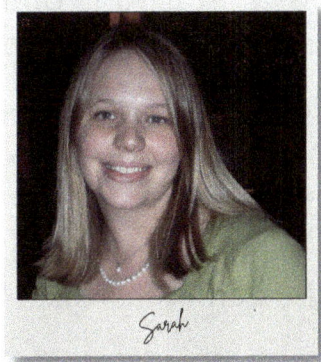

Sarah

Sarah Quips, "It was as if we had stumbled into that Garth Brooks song where he mentions he's 'got friends in low places.' We had been searching for God's community at the "Oasis." Cheesy, I know, but Mr. Brooks is from Oklahoma City, so it's fair game."

Ben went on, his eyes shining with passion, "We love and serve those outside the walls, but when we come together here, we celebrate what God is doing out there in our lives and in the lives of others. God wants to do something big here in this city." He was casting a vision to reach the entire city. He wasn't just trying to get butts-in-seats like some mantra from the movie Field of Dreams where if you "build it, and they will come." No, the view had an outward focus and celebrated what God is doing among His people. My mind was officially blown to bits!

It was strange, unexpected, and exactly what we needed—like finding the missing piece of a puzzle you didn't even know you were putting together. But we had yet to see if this was all talk-no-go or the genuine article.

Ben wasn't entirely done throwing us curveballs. He announced their outreach: handing out cold water at the local pride parade.

Wait!

Hold the phone!

I wasn't ready for this!

And it was on the hottest day of the year, no less. My mind reeled. This was light-years away from our comfort zone, farther than any church had ever asked us to go, and amidst a population of people I knew nothing about.

This was when Oklahoma City had never seen such a gathering of people, let alone even whisper such a thing.

> "The only example of Jesus that most of these individuals have seen was people yelling at them, with the Bible in hand," Ben explained, his voice soft but firm. "We want to show them who Jesus really is by serving and loving them the way Jesus would."

As he shared stories of simple acts of kindness building bridges of understanding, I felt something stir. It was subtle, like a whisper in the wind, but unmistakable: the Holy Spirit gently nudging us towards something new, something real, a part of God we had not yet seen or experienced.

Sarah squeezed my hand, and I knew she felt it too. We'd walked into this defunct grocery store looking for a church, but we might have found something even better - a chance to actually "be" the church. But what did that even mean!?"

As we left that day, the Oklahoma sun beating down on us, I couldn't help but laugh. Who would have thought that our search for genuine faith would lead us from the polished halls of a seeker-driven church to an abandoned supermarket? But then again, God does have a sense of humor. And apparently, He also has a thing for repurposed retail spaces.

SUMMER

Chapter Four

HOT PARADES COOL SHADES

THE DAY OF THE parade dawned with intense, mind-numbing heat, making you wonder if the sun had a personal vendetta against Oklahoma. Sarah and I joined our new church group on a family's front lawn, and Sarah said we were "armed with enough icy water bottles to hydrate a small army." Excitement, terror, and a lot of "what have we gotten ourselves into?" all rolled into one.

The first parade-goers approached, eyeing us with suspicion and heat-induced desperation. I half expected them to ask if we were selling the water or trying to convert them on the spot. But as we offered the bottles with nothing more than a smile and a "Stay hydrated!", their faces morphed from surprise to gratitude.

With each bottle we handed out, something strange started happening. It wasn't just the ice melting - the walls I'd built around my heart also began to crumble. That sounds a bit cheesy, but these weren't the faceless "others" I'd been taught to fear or pity. They were a person who'd driven three hours to be here, another just trying to find a community to belong to, and yet another who just really, really needed some water before they passed out.

As the day wore on, I marveled at the power of this simple act. We were just there, offering cold water, yet it felt revolutionary. We weren't wearing matching T-shirts with our church logo or handing out tracts disguised as $100 bills. No. We didn't have a fancy booth or a slick sales pitch. We just had water, smiles, and a willingness to be there. God seemed very present on that front lawn as we stepped out in faith. God appeared to do the rest as He stirred all of our hearts.

People notice! They started asking questions, not because we were shoving answers at them, but because they were genuinely curious. "Why are you doing this?" they'd ask, and we'd shrug and say, "Because it's hot and everyone needs water." Simple. It was like we'd stumbled upon some profound secret: sometimes, loving your neighbor is as simple as ensuring they don't die of heatstroke.

They began asking for prayer and if they could go to our church. I barely even knew the address to tell them where the old, smelly building was. I didn't exactly want to ask them to go to the old, broken-down grocery store either. What was happening!? Was I witnessing something like a miracle? Was this what Scripture discussed, where God would tug on people's hearts and draw them to Himself? I had so many questions.

They could sense something different. Somehow, they were encountering the collision of a little piece of heaven meeting with a little piece of earth.

We could sense that Jesus had much more in plan. He wanted to reveal more of himself through us, his "hands and feet." God's word was coming to life in and through us. Such a strange feeling.

Standing there, another water bottle in hand, I felt something shift inside. It was like a hunger that suddenly woke up and started growling. I wanted more of this. More of whatever this was that made me feel more alive than I ever had in years of sitting in air-conditioned church seats.

As Sarah and I drove home that evening, exhausted, sunburned, and smelling like we'd been marinated in sweat, we couldn't stop grinning at each other like idiots. We'd found something real and raw and a little scary. Our journey wasn't over - heck, it felt like it was just getting started. But for the first time in forever, we thought we were on the right path toward something that looked like what we read in Scripture.

That night, as we collapsed into bed, too tired to even brush our teeth, don't judge, I couldn't help but wonder what God had up His sleeve next. What was in store? Pun intended. This couldn't be a one-time thing and then return to "church" as usual. We asked, "God, what are you up to?" Because if this was what being a church looked like, sign me up for another round. God was suddenly revealing more of Himself in small doses.

Chapter Five

GETTING SAUCED IN THE PASEO

WE HAD STUMBLED INTO this unconventional church. The idea that we could partner with God in His work was thrilling and daunting. We were standing at the edge of something huge, but our map might as well have been written in crayon for all the guidance it gave us. All those years of sitting through ear-tingling sermons? They hadn't prepared us for this.

Our hearts were on fire, burning for more of Jesus and His way of loving people. It was like the words in the Bible were now dancing off the page, waving their arms and shouting, "Hey! This is what we've been trying to tell you all along!" The mysteries of God were vivid and like going from a fuzzy image to high definition. Things were starting to become more apparent.

Coming down from our spiritual high, we were stuffing our faces with pizza at Sauced, a local pizza shop in the heart of the Oklahoma City Paseo arts district. Our new friend Ryan was there too, another person who had joined Ben in planting this old defunct grocery store church in Oklahoma City from Colorado. As we picked at the cheese strings hanging from our slices, we started yapping about our roles and what was next in this crazy story God seemed to be writing.

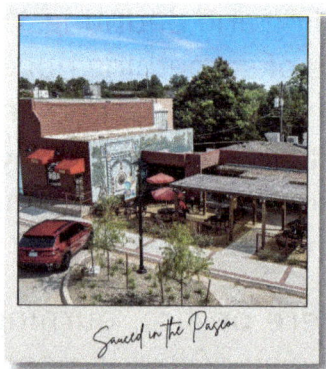
Sauced in the Paseo

That's when it hit me. I remembered this video I'd seen earlier - a guy in Dallas, Texas, serving hot dogs to folks down on their luck. But this wasn't your average "here's a hot dog, now let me tell you why you're going to hell" kind of deal. No, this guy had somehow sweet-talked the convenience store owner into giving him the soon-to-expire hot dogs.

He had this sign that said, "Turn or Burn." Before you roll your eyes, it wasn't what you thought. It was turning the hot dog, or it'll burn. Most people got the joke and had a good laugh. Only the folks who'd apparently left their sense of humor in their other pants missed it.

As I watched this guy serve up hot dogs and humor in equal measure, something stirred in my gut, and it wasn't just the pizza. This was the answer to our "what's next" question. It was so simple yet so profound: Love people, feed them, make them laugh, pray with them, tell them about Jesus. Boom. Gospel in action.

But let me tell you, the thought of actually doing it myself? Terrifying. It was like being asked to perform brain surgery when you struggle with Operation, the board game. This was way outside my comfort zone - it wasn't even in the same zip code as my comfort zone. Once again, we would be stepping outside into scary territory. But we knew this was the way forward.

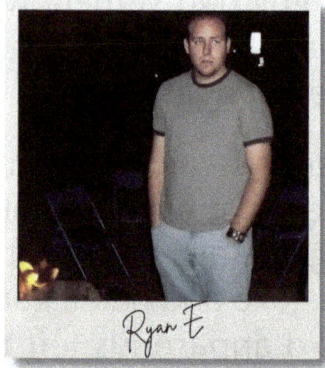

Ryan E

Ryan, bless his heart, must have sensed my internal freak-out. He whipped out this book, "Irresistible Revolution" by Shane Claiborne. The cover looked like it had been through a war. "This guy," Ryan said, "had faced the same stuff in Philadelphia."

Shane describes one point where he was itching to help so badly that he contacted Mother Teresa in Calcutta. Her advice to him was, "Come and see". So he did. His life was forever changed so much that he returned to the States and followed the prompting of God to help change his neighborhood. Needless to say, I was hooked!

Read it if you want a kick in the pants. It lit a fire under me to take that leap of faith. I don't agree with all of Shane's theological points, but his heart for loving others? That's the real deal.

Suddenly, I had a shining example. Someone who'd walked this path before and lived to tell the tale. I felt like I'd just discovered electricity or pizza without calories.

I couldn't wait to tell our newfound pastor. This was it - our next extensive outreach! God was about to take our little hot dog idea and turn it into a five-course meal of faith, love, and community that would change everything. Right!?

Chapter Six

TELL ME HOW IT WENT

Being so fired up about this revelation, I practically sprinted to meet Ben, our pastor-slash-barista extraordinaire, at the pizza joint the following week. I was ready to spill the beans, or the hot dogs, about this fantastic outreach idea. We'd already dipped our toes with the pride parade outreach! This was the logical next step in our "let's turn this city upside down for Jesus" movement.

Words tumbled out of my mouth, painting this grand vision of our church armed with tongs and condiments, ready to conquer the streets one hot dog at a time. But Ben? He just sat there, cool as a cucumber, and hit me with this zinger: "Tell me how it went."

Tell me how it went?

Wait, what!?

I blinked. Surely, I'd misheard. But nope, Ben just kept repeating it like it was his new favorite catchphrase. For a hot second, I thought he'd inhaled too much coffee steam during his last barista shift.

Then it hit me. This wasn't Ben being a wet blanket on our hot idea. He wasn't saying no - he was saying, "Go for it."

> I wasn't used to this. I was used to meetings to talk about meetings and form committees to have more meetings before anything was ever done. You know! The American way! "Ouch and Amen!" A little wink to our South African friends Mac and Naudine. Love you!

I'll admit, a part of me - okay, a big part - wanted to show Ben what he would be missing. Even though that one motive was about as pure as a mud puddle, something in Ben's challenge propelled us. God had given us this nugget of something. Ben thought it was a good idea; he was planting a church, and his hands were full. He would gather others to help pray for us as we ventured out.

So there we were, a bunch of regular people with more enthusiasm than experience, ready to take on the world... or at least the nearest street corner. We had no idea what Jesus would do with this motley crew, but we were ready to find out!

Chapter Seven

TONGS, WEAPON OF CHOICE

WE SET OUT! RYAN challenged us to set a hard date for our hot dog adventure the week before. And suddenly, we were - hearts racing, palms sweating, like Eminem on 8 MIle, standing in the middle of Walmart, loading grills and hot dogs like we were preparing for the world's most bizarre cookout.

Our destination? Downtown Oklahoma City—the part that makes your mom nervously ask if you're "sure about this, honey." As we drove towards what felt like the edge of our known universe, I couldn't help but shake my head at God's sense of humor. Armed with nothing but processed meat and misplaced confidence, we were ready to change the world—or at least feed a small part of it.

Once downtown, we realized we'd overlooked one tiny detail—where exactly were we supposed to set up shop? We kept looking at each other, hoping someone would suddenly develop a keen sense and know the perfect spot.

We pulled into the homeless shelter in that same area of downtown, in a stroke of what we thought was genius. Surely, they'd welcome us with open arms with our genius idea. Not so fast! "Three whole months of training," they said. We'd be eligible to serve sometime next century. I mean, these were hotdogs we were talking about. You'd think we were trying to hand out social security cards or the keys to Fort Knox, not a few frankfurters with some ketchup. There we were, a trunk full of hot dogs and nowhere to go.

We did what any sensible group would do—we found the most abandoned, sketchy-looking parking lot we could and started unloading. Nothing says "we're here to help" like lurking behind a run-down building with a car full of meat that you're pulling out of the trunk of your car.

Things got even more interesting. This tall, slim man starts yelling and walking towards us like we've just stepped on his turf. We froze. We were ready to throw down with our hot dog tongs, not exactly the weapon of choice for a street fight, but beggars can't be choosers. We were clearly out of our minds and out of our element. "Green," as some might call us.

He's getting closer and then yells, "Are you here to feed the homeless?" We're standing there, mouths hanging open, wondering how he could have known. Was it the tongs or the grill we had standing there?

It turns out that this was Quincy - or "Q" to his friends. He pointed us to a better spot and said, "You need to go over there." He points to a building that looked abandoned yet it had a certain charm and a large parking area next to a busy street. He continued, "You need to go over there where you'd actually be seen by the homeless." Being a homeless person himself, he would know. To add to the surreal nature of it all, he starts belting out worship songs like we're at an impromptu gospel concert. Poetic Psalms and praises he was making up on the spot. It was a beautiful moment, obviously orchestrated by Jesus Himself. C'mon Y'all!

From that moment on, Q became our unofficial guardian angel, keeping an eye on us as we struggled to serve this beautifully messy, utterly unpredictable group of people.

And just like that, our hot dog ministry was born - with a healthy dose of confusion, a splash of divine intervention, and more than a bit of help from our new friend Q.

Who knew processed meat could be the start of something so... holy?

Cue the Beatles song, "I get by with a little help from my friends, " minus the getting "high" part.

Chapter Eight

DROWNING CHARCOAL

In our new spot, standing to the side of a bustling street. Cars whizzed by, probably wondering if we were filming some bizarre cooking show. We didn't mind. People were honking because they were happy, right!?

We had our table set up, just waiting for God to send some hungry souls our way. Now, in the right place, poised for what God had in store.

We struggled to get the coals lit on our BBQ grill like it's some alien technology when this guy saunters up, declaring himself the "King of Lighting Grills." I didn't even know that was a royal title, but who was I to argue with royalty?

His Majesty gives us a masterclass in the art of drowning innocent charcoal in lighter fluid and tossing in matches. Let's just say we got schooled in the fine art of potential arson that day.

And Quincy was right, once we got those dogs sizzling, we'd rung the dinner bell for the entire neighborhood. People started appearing out of thin air - from under the highway, behind trees, places I didn't even know could hide a person. We had quite the eclectic crowd - some looked like they'd just stepped out of an interview, others like they'd been on an eight-day camping trip. Some faces were freshly scrubbed courtesy of the McD's bathroom, while others wore their grime like a badge of honor. But they all had one thing in common - a smile and a hankering for a slightly burned hot dog with a generous dollop of ketchup. Love was the day's special, and it was being served hot and fresh.

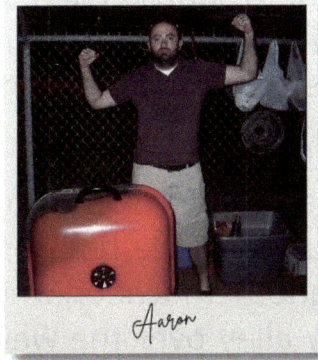

Aaron

We kept this gig going every Friday, riding high on the joy of this simple yet profound way of showing love and connecting with people. The connections were raw yet genuine. No fancy theology degrees were required, and no stuffy traditions to follow. Just us, some hot dogs, and a lot of divine intervention. We served up these delectable tubes of meat while praying for people, building relationships, and telling them the good news of Jesus' love for them.

All was going well and good, and we thought we had it all figured out when we were thrown our first curveball. The "enemy" didn't like us messing around in his territory, helping those that he so cunningly had placed in his hellish trap of poverty and mental illness.

The building owner showed up, probably wondering why his property had suddenly turned into an impromptu soup kitchen. We'd forgotten one tiny detail - asking permission. Oops. We had Q's permission, and that seemed enough at the time.

We promptly returned to square one, wondering where to set up our little hot dog ministry. We all looked for another location when Ryan pointed out a dusty alley over the way, across from the homeless shelter, "we should go there. It looks like a good place. It's complete with its very own dumpster." Classy, right? But hey, at least we had the homeless shelter's security cameras keeping an eye on us now. We were once again back in business, burning hotdogs!

Chapter Nine

MULTIPLICATION BUT NOT MATH

FOUR WEEKS INTO OUR little hot dog ministry, and let me tell you, we were meeting some of God's most... colorful creations. Each person had a story that could fill a book - or at least a fascinating pamphlet. One guy introduced himself as "Passing Through." He didn't want to get personal. He just wanted food. We just rolled with it like it was the most ordinary name in the world. When you're serving hot dogs in an alley, a guy named "Passing Through" is hardly the strangest thing you'll encounter.

Word started spreading through the homeless grapevine. Our little hot dog stand was becoming "the place to be." The crowds grew larger each week.

Our entourage also began to grow. We weren't the only ones hankering to serve others and find God among the down-and-out. People came ready to serve and see God move. This was before cell phones, social media, and other outlets to spread the news. If you wanted something to go viral, you would have to catch the flu.

At one point, Ryan said we should name the thing "Jesur-schnitzel" so that we could talk about it with others. He said, "Get it? It's mixing Jesus with a hotdog theme." It never caught on, but I still think it was clever—a dad joke, which I am very fond of.

We even had international representation. Among those showing up downtown were Jose and Samantha, who were fresh from Guatemala via California. While we were pushing hot dogs, they were slinging Cuban sandwiches and burritos they'd whipped up the night before, something they had been doing for several months at that point. I thought this was endearing, Americans slinging typical hotdogs and our Guatemalan friends slinging Cubanos and burritos. We were both doing what we knew.

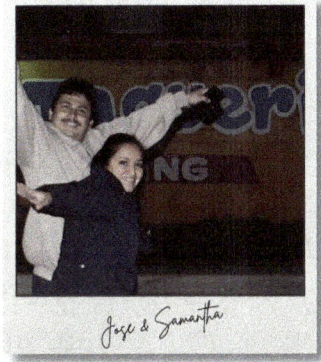

Jose & Samantha

I must pause and tell you about Jose and Samantha because they played a significant role in the rest of what took place.

Recently, speaking with Jose, he shared a remarkable story of how God guided them to Oklahoma. "Several months before you and I met," he recounted, "God strongly convinced our hearts to relocate from California to Oklahoma." He went on to explain how God had impressed upon them that He had something extraordinary planned through a combination of His scriptures and the testimonies of others. Even today, Jose holds a level of faith that is rare among most believers.

Jose and Samantha's hunger to witness God's power show up in ways found in biblical accounts led them to respond with unwavering faith. Within weeks of receiving this guidance, they took a leap and started a Bible study in their home.

Their obedience bore fruit quickly as the modest Bible study blossomed. Among the early people who participated in the Bible study was Caesar, whose life radically and rapidly changed. Caesar's encounter with God was nothing short of a miracle, igniting an immediate and intense desire to immerse himself in serving Jesus any way he could.

Caesar's dramatic conversion and eagerness to serve became a testament to the power of faith that had rippling effects on the lives of Jose and Samantha's Bible study. Caesar's story exemplified how one act of faithfulness could set in motion a chain of events that could impact an entire community, echoing the miracles they had been yearning to witness. As soon as we heard of their passion, we invited them to our little alley party.

Once they ran out of sandwiches and burritos, they met up with us next to the dumpster. But we soon ran low on dogs, and the line of hungry folks wasn't getting any shorter. Jose suggested we make a mad dash on a hotdog run. So off we went, two guys on a mission from God to buy processed meat, buns, and more ketchup at a small local discount grocery store about a mile away.

We combed the isles to find the big packs of hotdogs. Trying our best to hurry back. Jose swooped in like a lion pouncing on its target at the checkout and paid for the dogs. He said he was about to show me a "Biblical principle."

Now, I was used to Biblical principles being preached "at" me, not demonstrated in the middle of a grocery store checkout line. I was curious because I had no idea what Jose was talking about. I resisted a little. I wasn't used to people paying for me, but I just smiled and nodded this time because we needed to return quickly before everyone left without being fed.

Jose is a faith-filled heavyweight. The guy doesn't know how to pray without expecting God to answer. It was like he had a direct line to the Almighty or something. He said, "Today, I will buy you 30 hot dogs. Next week, you'll give me 300." God's math differed from ours, but this seemed like next-level Kingdom calculus. I didn't know where these mysterious hot dogs would appear, but I was glad to have enough to feed the rest of the crowd.

As we headed back to feed our hungry throng, my mind spun. How exactly was God going to pull off this hot dog multiplication miracle? Was this going to be a Biblical loaves and fishes type of deal? Especially since I was about to be as broke as the people we were feeding.

Chapter Ten

THE CREEPY WAREHOUSE

THE FOLLOWING WEEK, I was newly jobless. We began wrapping up our little hot dog extravaganza for the day, swapping stories about the day's adventures, knife fights, lover's quarrels, and the occasional slap fight - you know, just another day at the office when Ryan gets this wild hair to check out the supposedly abandoned warehouse across the street from the homeless shelter on the north side. I have no idea what gave him this wild hair, but already, by this point, we were feeling brave - or slightly unhinged. After seeing a few knife fights, what's a creepy old warehouse?

Ryan disappears for a bit, and we're half expecting him to come back with tetanus or a ghost story. Instead, he bursts back with news that's got him grinning and slightly fired up!

Ryan reports, "The warehouse owner, 'Tim, I think is his name,' decided to move to Oklahoma and turn the place into a ministry base" a month after we had set up camp next to the dumpster. We were excited, sure, but also a bit cautious. God was moving, but we weren't sure how this connection might go. Were we all just a bunch of lunatics out there seeking a movement of God?

This brick and steel, monochromatic, two-story warehouse monstrosity was lovingly referred to as "Satan's Stronghold" by the local homeless population. It had a rap sheet longer than a chili cheese foot-long hot dog. The cops rarely showed up in this area, even when a call went out. It was terrible news.

Tim U

The owner, Tim, was still in California while his friends were trying to flip properties in good ol' OKC. He had plans to do the same before God called him to change plans. However, in Tim's absence, this warehouse had turned into a veritable crime buffet - drugs, prostitution, you name it. It was like someone had decided to recreate Sodom and Gomorrah in downtown Oklahoma City.

Ryan tells us he met this other guy, Ryan K because all Ryans are drawn to abandoned warehouses apparently.

Ryan K was tasked with trying to coordinate with the police to clear out the place and get it ready for ministry. The only problem? They needed an idea of how to start a ministry in an abandoned warehouse, something none of us had any experience in doing.

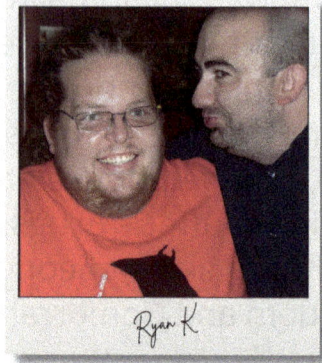

Ryan K

Here we were, slinging hot dogs in an alley, and suddenly, we were being offered a permanent place to minister. It was like going from a food truck to a five-star restaurant overnight. That next week, we packed up our small alley operation and set up shop on the front sidewalk of the slightly scary warehouse.

The sidewalk area, with its own parking spots, had enough room to grow, with the added benefit of still having the homeless shelter cameras pointed our way, just in case anything "went down."

I knew Ryan K from back in the day when we used to hang out at this Christian coffee shop called Outer Cafe and go to Cornerstone Festival.

Outer Cafe has enough miracles from Jesus to fill its own book. Good times, man, good times. Ryan K was and still is a man after God's heart. He is the gatherer of all gatherers and loves when people meet Jesus. It is his passion. That and art, music, and tobacco pipes.

As Ryan K gathered people and with a growing army of volunteers willing to brave downtown OKC and a new home base that looked like it could use an exorcism and a clear sense that God was up to something big, we had a renewed sense of adventure and hope. Things started to heat up even more than they had already.

Chapter Eleven

SYSCO FOODS, CASIO TUNES

SARAH AND I HAD been funding our hot dog venture out of our pockets. Suddenly, we were facing the real possibility that this whole thing might come to a screeching halt due to our finances quickly draining each week.

The thought of letting everyone down that we'd been loving and serving weighed heavily on us. We had enough for one more round of hot dogs - that was it. In a bittersweet gesture, we decided to splurge on extra ketchup for what we thought might be our last hurrah.

All week, I dreaded breaking the news to everyone who had gathered so faithfully each Friday. We'd built great relationships with the people we served and those who served alongside us. The idea of it all ending like this was agonizing.

Friday evening eventually rolled around. We loaded up and headed out to meet the homeless and face all the others who had been so dedicated to serving. Yet, we were in for another surprise.

As it unfolded, the scene was nothing short of amazing as we were struck by another miracle that God had so faithfully planned well in advance! It was like watching the book of Acts, where the Christian church had begun so many years ago, and the book of Corinthians, where we see everyone pitching in with various gifts. Things were coming to life right before our eyes. Everyone had something unique to offer - some served, others prayed, and a few even broke out in worship songs. People started bringing leftovers from their workplaces - coffee from "St. Arbucks" and bread from nearby chain bakeries. Some folks even brought tables and chairs, turning our little gathering into a proper community dinner.

Just as we were taking all this in, a blue sedan pulled up and out stepped a gentleman named Kim, blown away by what he saw.

Before meeting with us, he asked God to show him where to get involved in the community. Apparently, he'd just followed divine GPS to our little sidewalk gathering. "I turned where I felt God was leading," he said. "Turning right, turning left, and then God led me here." This was astonishing as we hadn't broadcast our location to anyone, with no fliers saying, "Hey, if you want to help sling hotdogs at homeless people in front of a creepy warehouse, then come down to the sketchy part of town." Nothing of the sort! We knew God gave directions, but not like this.

As it turns out, Kim was a distribution manager at Sysco Foods, a well known nationwide food distribution company, and offered to help us provide whatever food we needed. Later the following week, he gave me a tour of the facilities at Sysco Foods and introduced me to a few of his co-workers. Psst, I asked if Kim had any open positions available. He smiled and said, "Not at this time." Hey, I tried! That following Friday, Kim and I loaded my car with hot dogs, condiments, and water - three box loads of hotdogs totaling 900 hot dogs. More than anything you could ask or imagine, with chili on top!

We had no trouble feeding the homeless that night. God had shown up and shown off, completely dismantling our doubts about His provision. We fed around 400 people that day and had over 300 hot dogs left. Jose had just finished on his side of town.

Right on cue, Jose showed up, asking if God had provided the 300 hot dogs he needed to feed another group of hungry people.

Then it hit me! I remembered going to the grocery store with Jose when he heard from God that God wanted to rain down blessings of "footlongs" from above. Jose's lesson about God's provision hit home like never before. This was heavenly math. Faith in action is what you read about in the Bible but seem to brush over because it's too difficult to fathom. How could Jose have been so sure unless he had honestly heard from God!?

Jose and Samantha would eventually continue their operations inside the warehouse on the bottom floor. Setting up chairs, they continued to the next group of hungry people in desperate need of a Jesus-sized demonstration and a teaching of God's love.

Samantha, with her unique gift of making people feel welcome even if it was in a worn-out warehouse. Jose, with his gift of teaching from years of being a pastor and his uncanny ability to plunk away on a children's Casio keyboard powered by a small karaoke speaker.

People were aroused to worship God amidst the ever-growing testimonies of salvations, and their lives changed as Jose interweaved testimonies with worship songs as if they were a living mosaic of praise to God. He was teaching us all how to participate in a worship service instead of merely being spectators, as we were so used to doing before this whole experience.

Jose and Samantha are a dynamic couple! Downtown OKC didn't know what had landed in this lonely part of the town. Jesus was building his church among the unhoused and a population with many addictions, a population no one had dared to reach because they didn't have anything to offer back, and they weren't exactly the typical crowd most churches sought to bring into the sanctuary.

Just as God had brought Jose and Samantha, God had continued bringing more people downtown; some would even drive as far as two hours away.

God's immaculate planning never stopped astounding us as He would continue to bring new people with gifts to offer as we continued rolling out burned hotdogs each week.

Chapter Twelve

REFRESHING FREEDOM

MORE PEOPLE FROM ALL over the city and various churches began to join us, drawn by the buzz surrounding the activities and a few more leaders Tim had gathered. Word was spreading fast. People would show up asking how they could help and fit in. Churches began donating their kitchens for cooking, resources, and time helping in various ways.

People often approached me, asking if they could pray for others or share words of encouragement with those in need. It felt a bit odd to me—permission? I thought no permission was needed for that. Sometimes, things get a little messy, like burnt hotdogs, and that messiness becomes a thing of beauty. I encouraged them to follow where God led them, a lesson that Jose and Samantha had taught us: to be guided by the Holy Spirit. We shared scriptures and stories about how Jesus builds His church and how the body of Christ comes together with its diverse gifts. We were experiencing the freedom to minister without rules and regulations. Occasionally, you could even hear people mention how fun it was. Fun is not something I would typically associate with any past experiences of the American church we all grew up with.

There was a refreshing sense of freedom. We experienced the guidance of the Holy Spirit without the constraints of a rigid traditional hierarchy, and it felt liberating. Jesus clearly controlled everything around us as He drew more people in. It was remarkable how things seemed to fall into place each week.

It was vital during this time to take a page from our water bottle outreach at the parade - no branding, no fancy names, just simple love and service. This stood in stark contrast to the culture around us that seemed bent on slapping a logo on everything that moved to gain profit and recognition. We were moved by how Jesus took a group of people piece by piece and placed us together in a tapestry, calling to His goodness.

We started seeing God as a great conductor, moving his arms while the orchestra would play. Ryan E recalled a dream he'd had before coming to Oklahoma while still in Colorado. "I saw this large church gathering where the stage wasn't dominated by celebrity pastors." Which seemed a growing phenomenon. Ryan continued, "Instead, individuals came forward one at a time in an orderly manner to share what God had placed on their hearts." As we witnessed our community come together this way, it was as if the dream Ryan had was unfolding right before us. Nothing was centered around one personality or person holding all the sway of what was happening, except for Jesus, who seemed to be gently leading the whole procession.

However, the personalities we did notice were that of the homeless population as more of that tapestry began to show. We got quite the show, especially one Friday when one guy thought he lost his sunglasses, but we thought he may have lost more than that at some point.

Chapter Thirteen

ANGRY SUNGLASSES GUY

WHEN I RECENTLY CONTACTED Ryan E, curious if he had any stories tucked away from our hot dog ministry days. He remembered the guy looking for his sunglasses. He recounts:

> "So there we were, another Friday rolled around; Ryan K and Marsha, Ryan K's mom, came barreling up to us. Ryan K starts going on about how he'd been reading the Bible about the Israelites and Jericho. You know, the whole 'march around the city, blow your trumpets, and the walls of the city will fall, deal."

Marsha was convinced God was giving us a wink and a nod to walk around the warehouse and pray for God's protection. Thankfully, no trumpets were required and no walls fell.

Ryan continued, "So there we were, doing our best impersonation of the Israelites, walking in loops around the building, passing each other as we walked in different directions. Did we feel a bit silly? Yes. Did we do it anyway? Heck yeah!

At first, nothing seemed to change. It was business as usual - serve food, share Jesus' love, repeat."

But we were in for a surprise that would make even the most skeptical among us raise an eyebrow.

"Remember 'Angry Sunglasses Guy'?" Ryan asked. How could I forget? This guy was a regular in our little drama, always accusing us of grand sunglasses larceny. We'd even tried to give him a pair of ours once, but he batted them away like they were on fire. He was having no part in it. He wanted his glasses.

"He comes storming up like usual," Ryan says, "but this time, something weird happened. He gets to the spot where Marsha and Ryan had drawn a line where we'd been praying, and bam! It's like he hits an invisible wall. No kidding - it was like watching the world's angriest mime. We're all standing there, jaws on the floor, wondering if someone slipped something into the hot dog water. We never saw him again after that."

As Ryan recalled this scene, I remembered God seemed to be in the little things. He cares about our safety. Faith was becoming more interactive. We acted on God's prompt to pray, and then He showed us why He had prompted us to pray around the building. God showed us what it meant to be faithful even when our lives might be at risk.

We wanted to see if others were experiencing similar things. So we asked others if God was giving them any other prompts as we shared what happens when we obey God's nudges. This seemed to light a fire in all of us. Stories of God's provision, healing, and goodness started pouring in from everywhere.

Chapter Fourteen

HEALING

MARSHA HAD SEVERAL STORIES, one of which was a powerful story about their experience on one of the Friday nights. She said that she and Ryan found themselves in a particularly moving encounter with a man who called himself "Music Man." Despite his challenges, he approached them with a vibrant spirit and asked for prayer to restore his hearing.

As they gathered around him, Marsha noticed the signs of hardship etched on his face, including "cauliflower ear" from years of neglect, which told stories of battles fought, lost, and endured. He wore old, dirty hearing aids that hinted at his long-standing struggle with hearing loss.

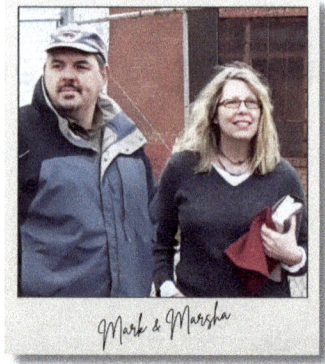

Mark & Marsha

With a sense of purpose, they joined hands and prayed fervently for Jesus to heal him. After the prayer, Marsha whispered softly behind him, and to her astonishment, he turned his head slightly and responded! It was a miraculous moment where he could not hear even the slightest sound before he could suddenly hear her whispering voice, even among all the noises of the busy street. Everyone praying for him leaped excitedly and couldn't help but belt out, "Praise God!" It was a powerful reminder that when we reach out in faith, things move and demonstrate hope where there typically isn't any.

Marsha also recounted a memorable evening. She told me the atmosphere was lively as the sun dipped below the horizon. The sidewalk beamed with laughter and the tantalizing aroma of grilled food. Amidst this warm gathering, her husband Mark began strumming his guitar, filling the air with beautiful melodies that drew people closer.

As he played, a man approached and took a seat beside him. They had an unspoken connection as if the music had invited this stranger into their circle. Mark generously offered the man a chance to play his guitar. Surprised by this unexpected kindness, the man accepted with tears streaming down his face. He began strumming a few chords—an emotional release that spoke volumes about his past. It turned out he hadn't played in years, and at that moment, the music unlocked memories and feelings that had long been buried within him.

This simple act of sharing music transformed the evening into something truly special. Everyone watched in awe as this man rediscovered a part of himself that had been absent. It was like a child had found his family after being separated for so long. This poignant moment transcended barriers, bringing joy in the most unexpected circumstances.

Through these experiences, God was restoring a healthy, sacrificial community among people striving for connection and empathy. More individuals continued to share similar nudges from

God, revealing His plans to show Himself even more as our humble gathering grew. People braved their way downtown.

Chapter Fifteen

CHURCH KEYS

AMANDA, ONE OF THE newcomers, felt comfortable enough to come downtown alone and jump in wherever she could. She had a natural gift for hospitality, which we would eventually discover is a central theme found in scripture. It could also be found in front of the warehouse as a gift pivotal to God's plan for ministering to others.

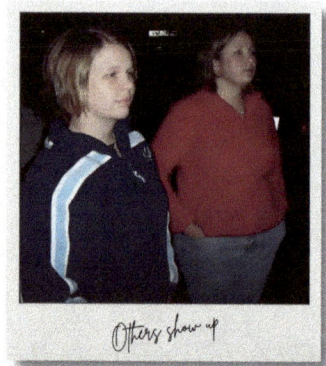

Others show up

Before long, she shared something she felt God was showing her. She had seen some prayer movements in churches and college campuses nationwide online. "God is moving in prayer and intimacy with His people everywhere," she said. We started noticing people passionate about prayer coming to Oklahoma and nearby states, and a few of us encouraged Amanda to follow what God was leading her.

We recognized this as a missing piece, so she began organizing prayer times. Others joined in, seeking God's presence on behalf of Oklahoma City. People began repenting, crying out to God regularly, and inviting others to do the same.

It felt like God's favor continued to rest on us during this time. We started experiencing grace with Him and with other leaders in the area. Church leaders began showing up at our hotdog grilling gatherings on W. California Ave, handing us keys and inviting us to pray in their churches. Yes, I know it sounds unbelievable, but a few of us ended up with keys and a list of addresses. We didn't fully understand why this was happening, but we were committed to following through just like we had when we first stepped onto that street, eager yet inexperienced. We dove in head first.

One such church that welcomed us was Bridgeway Church, a local church on the North East side of the city, which gave us access to their back room with a cozy coffee shop vibe with couches—perfect for college gatherings.

One evening, about 20 to 30 of us filled that space excitedly but unsure what to do next. Ryan and I quickly grabbed some pencils and paper because we had a unique idea for the night. We wanted everyone to write down what they were hearing from God. This was a bold move, but one we felt was where God was leading. After a few worship songs, we spread across the room to find our spot on the carpet. We sat quietly for what felt like ages, and then it happened. You could hear soft sniffles across the room as God touched hearts. There were moments of surprise and even laughter—God's presence was unmistakable, like a weighted warm blanket or a thickness in the air. His Holy Spirit seemed to move around the room and, at times, even fill the room. People were energetically writing.

After 20 minutes, we pulled together a circle of couches to share what we had written. What started as one person shyly sharing turned into an outpouring of confidence as more people opened up about their time with God. Excitement fueled the time of sharing. A beautiful message began to emerge: God's heart for restoration in relationships filled the room.

He wanted healing among us and unity within the church. Some even shared personal messages they felt led to give directly to the person God laid on their heart.

God had given me a word I wrote down for another person. I wasn't sure who this person was, but the message was clear. This individual had been deeply misunderstood and wounded in a relationship, leading to experiences of rejection.

As things started to close, one of the young girls with us stood up as if to leave, but she lingered, hoping to catch someone's eye and make a connection. After a minute, she headed for the door.

During this time, I felt God nudge me to give her the folded piece of paper on which I had written this message. I was too nervous to give it to her, fearing that I might have heard God wrong and would simply embarrass myself if I dared to hand her the paper. I tried bargaining with God, saying, "If she came back in, I would deliver the message to her."

There was no sign of her returning for a few minutes, which relieved me. But dang it, she appeared in the doorway for one last glimpse to see if she could connect before heading home. I stood up, took the long walk to the door, handed her the message, nervously cleared my throat, and said, "I think God may want to encourage you."

She stood there for what seemed like forever, reading the note. Immediately, she began weeping. I wasn't sure what to do other than call one of the ladies to come and help. I was out of my depth. I was later told that the message was spot on. She was contemplating whether to leave the church due to this misunderstanding she was facing. This word opened up an avenue for healing between her and the other person, spreading throughout the church for more restoration between relationships. Many of us had never seen anything like this, as God cares deeply for our relationships and the health of His church body.

We pulled together these written messages, delivered them to the church, and thanked them for their space. It was an honor to pray in that space and pray for the church.

As we continued this prayer journey, reports came in from other churches about relationships being mended and connections being restored.

God wasn't finished yet. God had shown relational and emotional healing; however, we were about to see another side of the power of prayer and intimacy as He would bring physical healing to our gathering that met in front of the downtown brick warehouse.

AUTUMN (FALL)

Chapter Sixteen

DIANE & JESUS IN THE WOODS

LEAVES FELL, AND THE cool winds of autumn began to blow in. We handed out warm jackets, hot cocoa, hotdogs, and burgers as Kim kept sustaining the ministry with generous gifts from Sysco Foods. Standing on the cold sidewalk, Marsha would gather people around our makeshift hobo heaters. This was nothing more than a metal barrel with wood and loads of lighter fluid to keep us warm. A trick we had picked up from the charcoal king from before.

Marsha would organize an improvised welcoming committee for the transient homeless new to our little shindig when a woman named Diane shuffled up for a hot dog. Diane was on the shorter side, but her presence was anything but small. She looked like she'd had a rough go of it – her hair doing its best impression of a bird's nest, and it was hard not to notice her right hand hanging limply at her side.

When we inquired, Diane shared her story. She'd been struck by a car three weeks earlier while in the throes of her heroin addiction. Too ashamed and under the influence to seek medical help, her hand had healed in a way that left it unusable and malformed.

Marsha and a few others quickly gathered to pray over Diane's hand with such intensity that we half expected an immediate miracle. But... nothing happened. It was a stark reminder that divine timing doesn't bend to human will.

Though Diane's hand remained unchanged, she didn't walk away without hope. She left with her spirit lifted, showered in a kind of love and care she hadn't felt in ages. This was akin to basking in a rare patch of sunlight for someone who'd gotten used to life's harsh coldness. Diane wandered back into the woods, returning to her tent-sweet-tent, carrying that warmth.

Next Friday rolled around like a leaf in the wind. Diane made an unexpected return. It was surprising because our visitors often drifted from one place to another. But there she was, waving her previously broken right hand in each of our faces, flexing her fingers open and closed with a grin. "Jesus healed my hand! He came to me and healed my hand!" with a glint, she was over-joyed!

Her hand was fully functional. The miracle had taken its time, but it had arrived as if to teach us patience and faith. Diane told us about a divine visitation from Jesus near her tent, transforming her life. We weren't sure if we could believe her due to her addiction, but one thing was for sure, her hand was healed, and we all got to witness it.

We stood there, amazed. It felt like we were stepping into some reality where the boundaries of faith stretched beyond our ability to compre-hend. Right there, in that humble setting, we witnessed a lesson in discipleship that was more impactful than any sermon. Jesus showed his love for this woman who had nothing to give. It was a vivid, living example of faith, hope, and the power of belief, even if it didn't take place in our timing.

We continued to see more of these lessons in love while serving in front of the warehouse. The chill of winter was looming, and we had to begin planning to go indoors if we wanted to continue loving this group of people. We had a desire to serve them as long as we could, or at least until they stopped showing up because they weren't "that crazy" when it came to getting a hotdog versus getting hypothermia.

Chapter Seventeen

WAREHOUSE FUNK

THE WINTER COLD HADN'T entirely set in, but it would appear every other week with bone-chilling winds. We were considering the possibility of being able to minister on the lower part of the warehouse once the vision of renovations had occurred, allowing us to escape the coming winter.

Tim, the owner of the building and a great visionary slash ad-hoc leader of this crazy gathering of people, would contact local churches, rallying them to join this ambitious renovation project that so desperately needed to take place. The building required open heart surgery to have the sweet smell of love and ministry take hold of its halls instead of being held by the smoky stench of desperation, blood, and a slight odor of the shadows of hell.

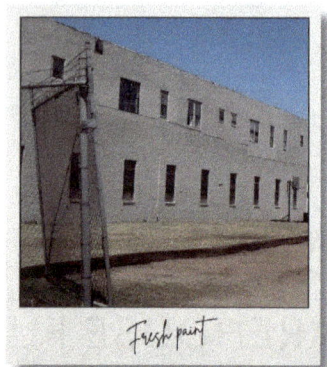

Fresh paint

The call resonated across the city with many, igniting a sense of purpose among those willing to lend a hand, from many churches and non-profits to individuals with a garage full of tools.

Tim made a call to the professionals. Police arrived swiftly, their presence a firm response to the thugs and racketeers who had previously taken residence on the upper floor. SWAT boots echoed through the halls as they cleared out the unwanted elements, restoring a sense of safety to the space.

Downstairs, on the first floor, a cavernous storage area overflowed with forgotten items haphazardly pushed to one side. The musty scent of decay mingled with something metallic and unsettling—a reminder of the building's troubled past. It was where shadows danced in the corners, whispering tales of lost souls and unfulfilled lustful desires.

The upper second floor revealed its secrets: rooms that once served as hideaways for crime, each equipped with small kitchenettes, now lay in disarray. The walls bore the scars of past conflicts, with streaks of dried blood telling stories of violence. One room still smelled of smoke and char, a grim reminder of a Molotov cocktail's destructive path. The kind of cocktail no one wants on a fun night out. Other doors were reinforced, their Jamaican doorstops rendering them nearly impenetrable during police raids. In one room still lay a horsewhip crop that undoubtedly wasn't used for livestock. The darkness lingered in every shadowy corner—a palpable weight in the air.

This building and its former inhabitants bore witness to chaos and hell. Each discovery deepened our resolve; we were not just restoring a building but reclaiming a space for hope and healing.

The sound of saws, hammering, and power tools urgently filled the air as the project began. Volunteers poured in as renovations kicked into high gear, armed with vigor and determination. Laughter and chatter filled the space as we worked side by side, fueled by the promise that this would become a new hub for missions training in Oklahoma City.

In those moments of labor, something profound began to unfold within us. We reflected on our lives as we scrubbed away grime and darkness. The weight of past tragedies hung heavy in our hearts, prompting us to seek forgiveness for what had transpired within these walls. New paint was being brushed on these walls, covering years of pain and regret, pain that started to fade away with each stroke.

Together, we embraced a journey toward redemption—an awakening that transcended bricks and mortar, breathing new life into the building and our spirits. We were once again renewed with purpose.

Chapter Eighteen

THREE DAYS OF PEACE

THE WAREHOUSE BEGAN TO take on a new form. Beams were reinforced, holes were filled, and fresh paint covered the walls. New sounds of hammers and brushes filled the air, marking a significant change in the building's atmosphere with a sense of pride and taking ownership.

Churches from various denominations across the city came together for a common purpose. Baptists, Pentecostals, Community, Methodists, Lutherans, and a few other denominations collaborated, putting aside their differences to focus on restoring the community. Plans were developed, ideas exchanged, and a vision for urban restoration emerged!

The rooms, once associated with illicit activities, were repurposed for good. Nonprofits moved in to focus on training for both inner-city and international missions. Tim and his family settled into the back larger corner room, creating an office space that would be a hub for this initiative. Others with mission experience also joined, bringing valuable insights.

News of the transformation spread throughout the city. Local officials began to notice and were intrigued by the positive changes within the warehouse that once laid as a blight on the town. Influential figures from nearby areas became interested in supporting this emerging center of hope.

Inspired by a desire to share their faith, a few people from Bridgeway Church and our budding group of Hot Dog serving "Jesur-schnitzels" proposed a continuous 24-hour reading of the Bible over a makeshift PA system outside on the East side of the warehouse. Volunteers eagerly signed up for shifts, ensuring Scripture would be read without interruption. The readings continued for three days and nights on a small makeshift stage.

When the last word from the book of Revelation was read, we received an unexpected report from the local police. During those three days of continuous reading, no crimes were reported within a three-block radius. This impressive outcome highlighted the powerful impact of faith and community engagement in transforming lives and neighborhoods.

We all had a renewed sense of how these words found within the pages of a Bible still held the breath of God; the very Spirit of God seemed to linger with each letter. City officials could not deny that something extraordinary had occurred due to this event as they would also comment on the sense of peace that seemed to linger in the surrounding area.

The building felt like it was finishing up, and things were moving smoothly. People came together for this purpose, and it was changing the hearts of everyone around...except for one person.

Chapter Nineteen

MONTHS OF TROUBLE

THEN CAME TROUBLE. A self-proclaimed whistle-blower emerged, claiming he was on a divine mission to halt our progress. His persistent interference became a bit of an irritation, as he reported what he believed were infractions to churches and local authorities, including the city Fire Chief. His primary claim was that the building didn't meet code requirements; he might have even suspected our faithful coffee maker wasn't up to snuff if given a chance.

Our momentum hit a pause. Tim was now looking at fixing the building's issues before we could get back to building a ministry hub and possibly finding a new coffee maker.

While churches had helped with initial renovations, we still faced significant problems—like the lack of fire sprinklers and the dubious effectiveness of the mini-split units. The estimated repair cost was over $100,000, exceeding any of our available resources.

Despite our attempts to move past the disruptions caused by this individual, he stuck around, spreading rumors and conspiracy theories, trying to throw a wrench in the vision. The motive behind his vendetta against our renovation efforts was a mystery. Maybe he really disliked our choice of paint. Perhaps the brand of coffee maker. Not sure.

We tried to have a constructive chat with him, but we were met with his firm belief that "the activities here were not of God" and that he "knew what God wanted for this area, and it seemed like no one was listening." Even though his approach was over the top, some of his complaints about infractions were actually valid.

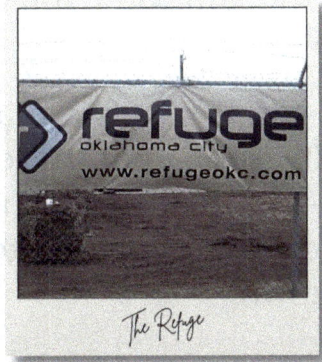

The Refuge

But Tim and all the people who had helped wouldn't give up easily. Tim's knack for finding solutions came to the foreground as he organized fundraisers with local churches and reached out to businesses, sharing his vision for what he was now calling "The Refuge," a mission training compound he believed with sincerity.

Tim arranged a fundraising event at a local restaurant, rallying support for the vision. This was the final effort to get the building up to code. I could see in Tim's eyes that evening the small glimmer of vision that was still left, mixed with a slight bit of nerves and the hope that God would pull off the miracle or miracles.

The community's support was heartwarming, yet we were still short of our target—until an unexpected donation from an anonymous benefactor closed the gap. God, indeed, did come through massively.

Installing the sprinkler system and fixing the mini-split units took months of hard work and patience. The delay was challenging but strengthened our determination to continue the mission downtown.

As for the "whistleblower," his impact gradually diminished. He grew quite the reputation for himself, having little, if any, influence in the city or with any of the officials, especially with the Fire Chief, who said the guy was a nuisance but had brought attention to legitimate issues we couldn't ignore.

The whistleblower may have gone on to start his own renovation project, perhaps with his favorite brand of coffee maker? Who knows?

This journey, though brutal, turned out to be a blessing. It was clear that God allowed for this occurrence so His grace would be revealed in the favor we gathered with the city officials. We came out of this trial with a fully compliant building ready to serve our community's needs. It brought our community closer, gave us a renewed purpose, and improved our relationship with city decision-makers as we worked together on compliance. We had earned the city's trust and support!

WINTER

Chapter Twenty

ROLL OUT THE TENT

WINTER WAS OFFICIALLY FULL-SCALE, and a dump truck of warm jackets and blankets was in dire need. Churches began sending groups to assist the homeless once again.

A notable event occurred one Saturday when a large mega church organized a "hugantic" ginormous gathering in the field on the East side of the Refuge. This event was to be a pivotal movement for the area. Everything was grand and well-branded. The signage and directions were well laid out.

This event, while well-intentioned, had mixed results among the homeless population, who seemed to be a bit confused about the situation. They weren't used to such fanfare in their honor.

The atmosphere resembled a carnival, complete with the aroma of popcorn, pastries, and various beverages. It was as if the Oscars, red carpet and all, had decided to host a show on the streets, and everyone was slightly unsure if they were the guests of honor or just stumbled upon a very elaborate upscale picnic.

Working with local authorities, they created a block party atmosphere. Services ranged from free shaves to clothing distribution and even photo sessions for ID cards. The goal was to provide dignity and potential employment opportunities for the homeless.

The setup was impressive. A mammoth outdoor clothes closet displayed neatly organized garments by type and color. Volunteers guided homeless individuals through the selection process, treating them with exceptional care and attention. It was the most exclusive shopping experience that didn't cost a dime. Gucci and Versace, step aside, there's a new trend in town, and it's called generosity.

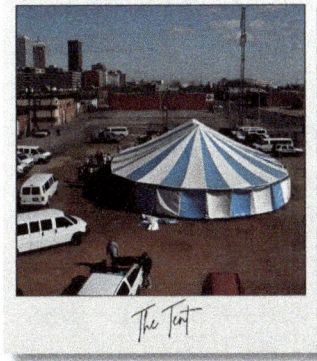

The Tent

A large tent, reminiscent of old-time revivals, was erected on Sunday afternoon to house a hot buffet and provide a space for worship and teaching afterward. There was a rush to organize the influx of people from all directions. Homeless individuals approached with a mix of excitement and wariness. They were eager to access the resources and hoped for lasting relationships from this grand event. It was like a spiritual buffet meets a TED Talk garnished with a hint of community spirit.

Volunteers greeted the individuals warmly, promising continued prayers and future visits once the event had concluded. For one whole weekend, the homeless felt valued and cared for. For one entire weekend, they received an outpouring of love and attention, filling them with hope for community and fellowship.

However, concerns began to surface. Some homeless individuals confided their uncertainty that these newfound connections might be short-lived. We couldn't fully grasp their apprehension at the time, having never witnessed such a grand display of care for this community. We couldn't comprehend their sad emotion as it seemed like this ministry was focusing all its attention on the people found in the pockets and shadows of the streets.

As the event ended, their uneasiness and anxieties were realized. By Sunday late evening, the church had vanished. The inflated expectations that were raised promptly settled back down to earth. The quick relationships and care faded, leaving a profound sense of loss.

One unhoused person expressed frustration, saying they were "used to people coming down and helping themselves to get their spiritual 'jollies off,' never to be seen again." This sentiment echoed the experiences of many living in the city's dark corners.

The genuine need revealed itself. People willing to stay beyond the initial excitement to build lasting relationships with those desperately seeking human compassion and connection were desperately needed.

Some of the church equipment and trash bins from the event were left behind, and they were going to be picked up later by a church crew.

Thankfully, they left their big tent behind.

Chapter Twenty–One

HEARING DIFFERENT LANGUAGES

LATER SUNDAY EVENING, WE had permission to use the tent, at least, until they came to pack them up. This provided some variety from the usual spot where we typically set things up in front of The Refuge. This also allowed for a space for teaching, complete with a comfortable carpeted stage.

Sarah recalls, "One evening after we had finished feeding those in need, the sun had set. Inside the tent, side-lights illuminated the space, creating a warm and inviting atmosphere. People began to gather for worship, prayer, and teaching. Over the many months Jose had built a steady following from within our community. Jose took to the stage with a small child-sized bullhorn that wasn't as loud as you would hope.

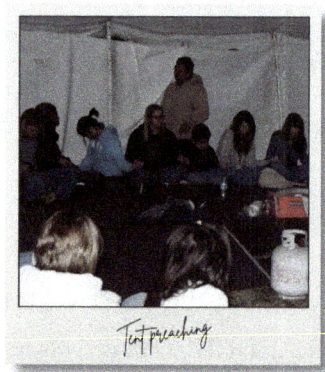

Tent preaching

Jose preached with passion and fervor in Spanish, his native language, making it easier to convey a deeper message. The crowd responded enthusiastically, shouting "Amen!" and encouraging him as he spoke. Jose's friend Caesar provided a basic English interpretation for those sitting close to the front, but I noticed a young boy lingering at the back of the tent. He was dressed head to toe in matching FUBU gear adorned with the Rhino logo. It was common for us to be on the look-out for suspicious characters or activities. It was something we had grown accustomed to over this time. At first, this kid seemed detached from what was happening around him. He was peeking in curiously but didn't engage with the worship or teaching. I remember thinking he might leave before anything significant happened. However, something remarkable did occur when Jose extended the invitation for an altar call. This young boy suddenly ran forward and dedicated his life to Jesus! We were all shocked as he hadn't shown any signs of being moved by Jose's message until that moment.

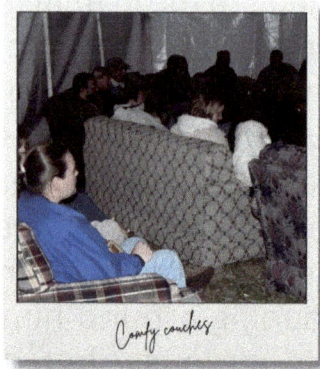

Comfy couches

After the boy committed his life, Jose asked him, "When did you learn Spanish?" The kid looked puzzled and replied, "When did you speak Spanish?" It was at that moment that we realized something extraordinary had happened. This young man had heard every word of Jose's sermon in perfect English! Despite Jose preaching exclusively in Spanish and the translator's voice being inaudible from where he stood at the back of the tent many rows back, God had miraculously allowed this boy to understand everything. This experience was new for us—beyond anything we had ever witnessed. It was a powerful reminder of God at work. We were left in awe of how God touched this young boy's life that night and continues to move among us in ways that challenge our understanding and deepen our faith. It reinforced my belief that no matter our circumstances or limitations, God is always at work, transforming lives and drawing people closer to Himself."

Even though we never saw him again, that being the nature of that population of individuals, Jesus continued to minister to him since he had such a unique welcome to his relationship with Jesus. Jose would follow up with that boy to see how he was doing.

We had many of these long evenings, and afterward, we would pack everything back into each of our vehicles and contemplate if we wanted to gather for a late-night meal together to recap the day. We just didn't want to go home after such exciting things like this had taken place.

Chapter Twenty-Two

BREAKING BREAD MEXICAN STYLE

FELLOWSHIP AND BREAKING BREAD were essential to keeping glued together for encouragement and vibrance.

"Samantha had told us of a great Mexican restaurant nearby," Sarah said, "which eventually became our usual suspect for a place to eat because it featured a fun zipline for the ticket orders that would be zipped across the restaurant as each order came in. That and a rice milk drink, Horchata. The smell of freshly cooked tortillas would make you wanna slap yo' momma!"

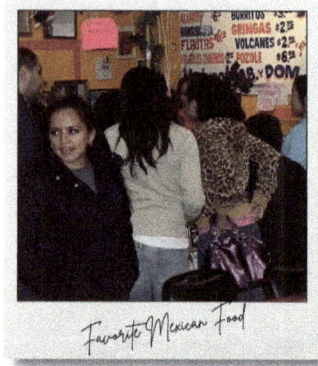

Favorite Mexican Food

As we pulled the tables together, there was a family atmosphere, and many of our people poured into this unsuspecting eatery. Some were ready to eat the freshly cooked Menudo, which I am not a fan of. Woe!

"In this semi-lit hole-in-the-wall," Sarah continued, "you could easily hear laughter, joy, and stories about what we had witnessed God do while serving food and prayers. People would recall the names of those who they served. These homeless vagabonds were becoming our friends. We heard their stories and were moved to help however we could."

These were such sweet times of fellowship and filling our faces with good Mexican food. We would marvel at how God had brought this diverse group of people together for such an occasion.

Some of those stories we would share were of people being helped to get jobs and places to stay to help them get back on their feet. Jose was even asked by a couple who had met on the street to help officiate their wedding ceremony. Excited about the prospect of seeing a wedding from this population of people, we promptly went into action!

Chapter Twenty-Three

STREET WEDDING

A FEW WEEKS PASSED, and this newly formed family—a blend of unhoused individuals and those eager to help—gathered at a local church hall.

Street Wedding

Samantha and several other women transformed the space beautifully. There were doilies everywhere, more than you'd see in a snowstorm, and the sanctuary was filled with the delightful scent of vibrant flowers. With sheer joy and excitement, the couple exchanged their vows.

We all cheered as this relationship, which had begun on the streets, blossomed into a beautiful marriage. It felt like a powerful symbol of what God was doing in the streets of Oklahoma.

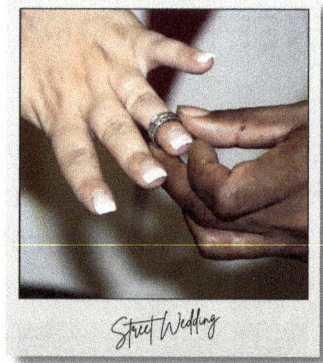

Street Wedding

Being part of such a moment filled us with happiness; it felt like we were truly making a difference in the lives of those around us. No one was left unchanged, and we experienced more moments like this as time passed.

We began to realize that simply feeding people was becoming less important. What was truly needed was consistent fellowship with the folks on W. California Ave. While we still planned to provide meals, we decided to focus more on building genuine relationships as our efforts continued to grow.

Chapter Twenty–Four

WEDDING FEAST FOOD

ON ONE OF THE coldest nights we had up to that point, Ryan K's dreads began to freeze up, and Sarah and I wore several jackets, almost looking like that kid in the movie A Christmas Story. Ryan E was roughing the cold because he was "from Colorado, and this was nothing." We had to fire up the hobo heaters once again. This time, it's extra hot. I just bought more lighter fluid. We sat on our couches that had somehow shown up in front of the warehouse, courtesy of our friends from the woods.

We found ourselves alone, as few people were brave enough or even dumb enough to venture outside in those temperatures. Only a few homeless would come out for some of our homemade hot cocoa and coffee.

We stayed long enough to see if any individuals needed food or warmth when Ryan K decided to mention that he was hungry. We all felt it, but it was Ryan who broke the silence. One of us piped up and semi-snarky said, "Maybe we should pray that God will bring us food." We were shivering and wanted to go somewhere warm, but we had committed to seeing this through and maintained that we were there for the homeless.

Ryan K prays the most sincere and somewhat desperate prayer I've ever heard. We knew God worked in His timing and some of the strangest ways, but we half expected to see the answer to this prayer come through the following week, not immediately. Many business owners were even getting the hint that it was too cold to keep anybody out by closing and sending their workers home.

Fifteen minutes when a large stark white van out of the nineteen eighties showed up and stopped hurriedly right in front of us. Some of us thought to ourselves, "Welp! This is how I get kidnapped".

A man and woman came, rushing out to open the side van door, and asked if we wanted any of the "wedding feast" from the ceremony they had just catered. I'm sure we looked dumb as none answered initially because we couldn't understand what was happening.

God had delivered in every sense of the word! This wasn't just any type of food that was being thrown out someone's window right at someone's poor, homeless, unsuspecting face like usual. No, this was food from the Wedding Feast.

God had brought us wedding food, the finest food there is. We fed ourselves plump and still had some to take home with us. Once again, God never ceases to awe us with His love, and he heard our desperate, shivering, cold prayer on that blustery, frigid night.

The cold continued, and the homeless population dwindled because they knew better than to be out in the ice wind. Apparently, we didn't. Nope, we would just bring more hot cocoa next time.

Chapter Twenty-Five

STIRLING PIES

As OKLAHOMA CONTINUED ITS tirade of cold wind that would blow through layers of clothing and send a chill up your spine, we decided to take a night off from serving downtown and have some fun together the following week.

As Ryan E, Sarah, and I sat at our house, none of us could come up with anything fun to do as most things were shut down or held indoors at private parties.

While making hot cocoa for ourselves, it hit us. A blowout sale was going on at "Worst Buy." We knew this sale line would stretch past all the connected shops and even wrap around the building. Hot cocoa would come to the rescue, and we would be the ones to serve it, hoping to connect with someone who we could talk with and even pray for.

We hunted down every thermos in the house and filled them with piping hot cocoa. We were armed with marshmallows, ready for action. As we popped in the car and drove down, we found a tent city and lawn chairs where people were camped out, waiting for the big box store to open their doors. Some were thankful we had a hot beverage for them to sip on, while others were a bit more reluctant. One lady even shouted that she thought we were trying to hand out drinks just to make everyone have to pee, hoping it would shorten the line as people dashed off to the restroom! That would have been a brilliant plan if we wanted to be first in line for the giant flat-screen TV on sale for half off. No, we just wanted to make some people smile and possibly have an encounter with Jesus.

While going down the line, we met a young man named Sterling. He seemed out of place and a bit nervous. He didn't have a lawn chair or a sleeping bag. He was just crouched down, playing hokey pokey with one leg in and one leg out, not really committed to the consumer line. He said he wanted to serve as God led him. He went on to explain, "I sensed that God was urging me to show love to the people waiting in line, so I brought out some pies my dad had baked today." He pointed to several pies in a few shopping bags, chocolate, apple, and pecan. He said, "Honestly, I had been too shy to hand them out myself. I was waiting for a sign or hoping someone else would join me to make that first move."

Here it was! Evidence that God was working in the hearts of people all over the city, and we were fortunate to have "bumped" into Sterling. What are the odds? I mean, really? This was un-believable! God seemed to be everywhere, even in the retail line of desperate shoppers.

Sterling fired up as he joined us, handing every-one hot cocoa and pie. People seemed aston-ished that we had prepared a treat for them. We prayed with a few people as we went along, but overall, God had shown His creativity in such a mind-boggling way. He showed us His greater community in pockets all over Oklahoma City.

Winter had come and gone, and now it was time to break out the briquettes again and venture back downtown to meet our people and build back those relationships that might have faded a bit over the winter. Our hearts were warm, and our hunger to return to seeing God's community at work was heating up.

SPRING

Chapter Twenty–Six

EASTER FEASTER

THE WARM SPRING AIR finally chased the winter chill, and Oklahoma City was buzzing with newfound energy and activities. An extraordinary community blossomed in OKC's heart, drawing people from afar. Now that it was warming up, word would once again begin to spread like wildfire, reaching as far as Stillwater OK the home of Oklahoma State University, where a group of college students, who had been meeting for years in a college residence hall, decided to make the two-hour journey to witness the excitement firsthand.

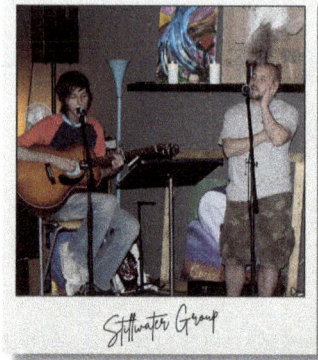

Stillwater Group

Their willingness to travel from so far had sparked a movement spreading across that part of the state. One of these college student leaders said it looked like "The downtown area had volunteers that outnumbered the homeless population."

God was drawing people of all ages and backgrounds to serve and witness His goodness and ability to bring change to a city that desperately needed it.

Easter time was drawing near. This diverse community commemorated the Easter occasion with a grand feast, inviting new friends and the homeless population to join.

Ryan K's dark-haired friend, known for her way with words, christened the event by calling it the "Easter Feaster," a name that perfectly captured the spirit of the occasion. She would go on to take the lead on organizing the event while pulling in helpers for each moving part. A true gift of administration and creativity.

Sarah and a group of dedicated women from local churches took charge of the culinary preparations, determined to create a meal that would be remembered for years.

Inspired by a profound spirit of service, local churches—including New Covenant Christian Church a local church on the North West side of the city—opened their doors and kitchens again, thanks to the enthusiastic support of our newly furloughed missionary friends, Andrew and Sylvia. Their commitment to community outreach provided everything necessary to realize this ambitious vision.

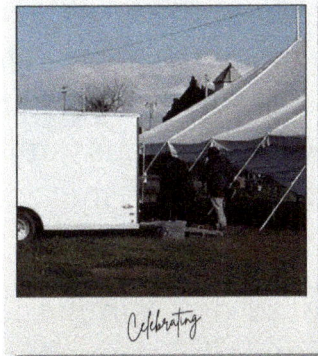

Celebrating

The collaboration among these churches created a vibrant atmosphere where generosity and compassion flourished, ensuring no detail was overlooked in the preparations for this special event. Seasoned cooks eagerly shared their cherished family recipes, seeing this as an opportunity to show love to the city's often-overlooked segment of the community.

When Easter finally arrived, the field next to the Refuge was a flurry of activity as volunteers prepared for the special occasion. The tables were set with care, each place-setting a symbol of welcome. As guests began to arrive, they were greeted by the sight of tables ready for the occasion with tablecloths and place settings. As we unloaded vans and cars full of food trays, food started pouring in.

We spread the word to our friends living in the woods, emphasizing that everyone had a place at the table to enjoy the feast. The meal began with a heartfelt prayer, followed by the passing of plates filled with luxurious family-style dishes. As they ate, stories were shared, and connections became more evident.

What had started as a simple idea had blossomed into a beautiful tapestry of community, bringing together people from all walks of life to celebrate togetherness and compassion. We were being shown a window into God's idea of family. It was an abundant display of His love and goodness for every tongue, tribe, and nation.

Over our Friday even meals, as we finished serving, we often shared intriguing insights from articles or videos that had caught our attention throughout the week. One evening, a particularly striking story surfaced. It revolved around the subject of broken windows.

Chapter Twenty–Seven

FLOWERS & BROKEN WINDOWS

INITIALLY COINED BY JAMES Q. Wilson and George L. Kelling in 1982, the Broken Window theory suggests that a single broken window can create a chain of disorder in a neighborhood. The idea is simple: when a window is left unrepaired, it sends a message that no one cares, creating an environment where further vandalism and neglect can flourish.

Malcolm Gladwell resurrected this theory in "The Tipping Point," illustrating how small, seemingly insignificant details can dramatically influence social behavior. As we delved into this notion, we began to ponder its implications for our community.

The conversation deepened as we reflected on our surroundings—how a neglected space could spiral into disarray if left unchecked. We shared stories from our neighborhoods, recalling instances where small acts of care—or lack thereof—had made all the difference.

The concept of the broken windows sparked an intriguing thought, if small acts of neglect could lead to a downward spiral, couldn't the opposite also be true? We wondered if making small, positive changes in our area might have broader, uplifting implications. Though uncertain where to begin, we were eager to test this hypothesis.

Our opportunity arose unexpectedly when college students, inspired by the numerous church youth groups now working on larger community projects under Tim's guidance, began infusing the area with beauty. A group of determined young women took it upon themselves to plant flowers on a corner of the field—a spot notorious for less savory activities.

What followed was an unexpected battle for beauty. These resilient college women would plant fresh flowers weekly, only to be trampled and destroyed days later. This cycle continued for weeks, transforming into an unspoken turf war between those seeking to uplift the community and those resistant to change.

Despite the constant setbacks, the women's resolve never wavered. They returned week after week, replanting flowers with unwavering dedication. Their persistence symbolized hope and transformation for many of us watching from the sidelines.

Then, one day, something remarkable happened: the flowers remained untouched. The reason behind this sudden change was unclear, but it felt like a small yet significant victory. It was as if the persistent pursuit of beauty had finally overcome the forces working against it.

It showed us that persistent efforts to bring beauty and care to a neglected space despite repeated setbacks could eventually lead to meaningful change. The battle of flowers had become more than just about plants. It was a tangible example of how small, beautiful acts could have more significant, positive implications for our community.

The triumph brought about by these flowers would symbolize much more than just an appreciation for botany. Their beauty would significantly transform lives and soften the hearts of even the most hardened individuals.

Chapter Twenty–Eight

FLOWERS & DRUGS

As THE FLOWERS CONTINUED to thrive, curiosity grew about their unexpected survival. Tim shared a remarkable story that left even him, a seasoned minister, in awe.

One of the area's most notorious drug dealers approached Tim with a tale that highlighted God's sovereign and relentless pursuit of those He calls, underscoring the transformative power of small acts of beauty and persistence, showing how they can touch lives profoundly and unexpectedly, reaching even those who seem furthest from grace.

A slender man named Mike approached Tim, his gruff demeanor and weathered appearance telling the story of a life marked by hardship.

With frustration etched across his face, Mike exclaimed,

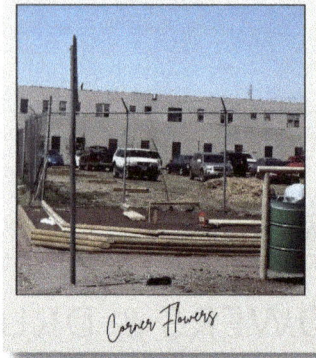

Corner Flowers

"These damn flowers keep showing up every damn week. I keep kicking them down. I'm getting sick and tired because I'm just trying to make a living. That's my corner! These damn flowers remind me of my daughter. I haven't been allowed to see her in years."

As he spoke, the weight of his words revealed a deep longing for connection—a flicker of the bond he once shared with his daughter before he fell into a lifestyle that now felt like a prison.

Tim didn't hesitate; he began to share the gospel with Mike. Over what seemed like a long discussion filled with many questions, Mike had accepted Jesus into his life. As he turned to leave, there was a noticeable shift in him; he puffed up slightly, his posture straightening as he briskly walked away. Yet, Tim could see the glimmer of tears threatening to spill from Mike's eyes, as if something monumental had just begun to crumble within him.

We recognized that this chance encounter with Jesus was genuine because what followed was nothing short of miraculous. In the following weeks, an abundance of spiritual fruit emerged from Mike in the form of outrageous generosity.

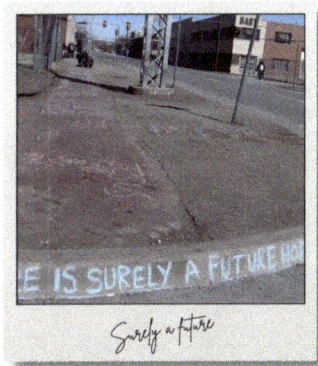

Surely a future

SUMMER

Chapter Twenty–Nine

NEIGHBORHOOD HOUSES

MIKE'S ENCOUNTER WITH JESUS sparked a profound change in his heart. As time passed, he engaged in numerous deep conversations with Tim, each peeling back layers of his hardened exterior. The transformation within Mike was so powerful that it led to an extraordinary act of generosity. Over time, he would eventually surrender the neighboring houses he owned, properties that had once been the epicenter of the area's drug manufacturing operations in that region of Oklahoma City.

This selfless gesture left us all back on our heels. Just weeks earlier, Mike had seemed so far removed from faith, yet here he was, demonstrating a level of generosity that none of us had ever witnessed, not even from among any of us. His actions were a testament to the radical change that had taken place in his life, showcasing the transformative power of his newfound relationship with Jesus.

Mike's decision to relinquish these properties wasn't just about giving up material possessions; it symbolized a complete break from his past life and a commitment to his new path. This unexpected turn of events vividly illustrated how genuine spiritual transformation can lead to tangible, life-altering decisions that impact the individual and the entire community.

The evidence of faith would continue to be seen all around, even in the daily lives of those who would attend in helping our friends from the dark corners of OKC.

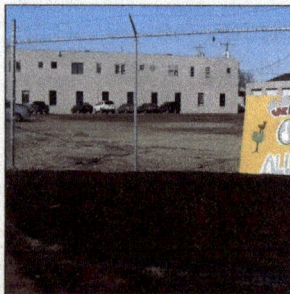

Corner flowers

.

Chapter Thirty

FAITH TO MOVE MTNS OF CREDIT

LIVES WOULD CONTINUE TO change even among those who were serving. Jose and Samantha's commitment to fostering a caring community among the local unhoused population faced an unexpected setback when their car spit and sputtered and finally said, "Nope." The mechanical failure threatened to disrupt their vital ministry work downtown, posing a significant challenge to their ongoing efforts in this urban area of need.

Undeterred, Jose declared with unwavering confidence, "Samantha and I will petition God for a vehicle through prayer." His remarkable faith often led him to seek the Holy Spirit, describing the experience as a "fire" coursing through his body. He firmly believed that God would answer any sincere requests he and his family brought before Him, patiently awaiting a response like a child anticipating a special delivery.

To everyone's astonishment, Jose and Samantha arrived the following week in a gleaming, gold-hued Mustang—a generous gift from a newfound friend. Samantha stepped out of the car in her high heels, radiating joy as she expressed her gratitude for God's abundant blessings. It was hard not to picture her as a princess stepping out of a chariot rather than just a couple from our neighborhood.

News of this extraordinary event spread quickly. Intrigued, Jose's friend Caesar approached him to verify the story. Caesar, who struggled with an unreliable van and amusingly poor credit, asked Jose for similar prayer support for a new car. With a grin, Caesar quipped that his "credit was so bad he should get arrested," prompting nervous laughter among the group as we all wondered, "Can bad credit actually land you in jail?" Jose prayed confidently and directed Caesar to a local car lot.

Later that week, just before closing time, Caesar visited the dealership to look at used cars. The hurried salesman informed Caesar that he would have to be contacted after a credit check. Deeply skeptical, Caesar was astounded when the salesman called early the following day with surprising news.

The salesman presented Caesar with an offer for a new car, citing an unexpectedly excellent credit score—higher than any he had ever encountered, even among most businessmen. It was as if Caesar's credit score had magically transformed overnight, leaving him wondering if he had accidentally stumbled into a fairy tale.

Remarkably, the new car payments were lower than Caesar's current payment for his unreliable van. He couldn't help but think that maybe his old van had been secretly plotting against him all along.

The following week, Caesar proudly arrived in his new vehicle, baffling everyone. As they gathered to admire the car's fresh scent and impressive features, Jose encouraged Caesar to share the good news of God's love for others as a testimony.

Things like this continued strengthening our faith and inspiring others to believe in the power of prayer and divine provision while reminding everyone that sometimes, even bad credit can lead to unexpectedly good outcomes.

Chapter Thirty–One

COMMUNITY ON MISSION

THE COMMUNITY WITHIN THE walls of the Refuge began to grow as home groups from various churches utilized the warehouse space for worship services and teaching times.

The warmth of glowing lights now filled the hallways and living spaces. The rooms that once were dens of all kinds of debauchery were now havens for mission-minded families praying and eating together regularly. Ministries of all kinds began to spring from this beige cinder block building.

Sarah and I reflected on our time on W. California Ave. We sensed that this chapter of our lives was drawing to a close. Our thoughts drifted back to a pivotal moment when we attended a festival called Cornerstone Fest in Illinois, a Christian music festival that had been going on since the 1980s. We first met another lovely mission-minded couple there and received profound advice about pursuing God.

They shared a powerful insight: "When God turns a corner, turn the corner with Him. Don't keep going straight; you might find yourself alone and without His grace."

It was evident that God had turned a corner as things began to wind down with the hotdogs ministry, and things started to shift more towards the ministry that was taking place inside the walls of The Refuge. This signaled the conclusion of a transformative chapter in our lives. As we looked back on our journey, an exciting realization dawned upon us—our next calling awaited in India, unfolding with the same divine orchestration that had guided us through our recent experiences.

Perhaps we wouldn't have been ready to hear God's voice for the next chapter if we hadn't fully experienced this last chapter. The chapters were inextricably linked and seemed to be building upon one another.

Our hearts overflow with gratitude for being part of this extraordinary narrative, witnessing lives unfold, and experiencing the outpouring of God's love into this community. Despite our challenges, we cherish every moment of those many months serving the diverse population in downtown Oklahoma City.

The setbacks we encountered only strengthened our resolve and deepened our faith. They were not obstacles but stepping stones, each teaching us valuable lessons about perseverance, compassion, and the power of unwavering belief.

As we prepared to embark on our new adventure to India, we carried with us the rich tapestry of experiences from Oklahoma City. The faces we had encountered, the lives we had touched, and the miracles we had witnessed will forever be etched in our memories, fueling our passion to continue serving wherever God leads.

THANK YOU!

I would like to thank you for reading this memory. For many of the people there, this was just the beginning of a lifelong journey.

Join us here: facebook.com/Homeless.Hotdogs

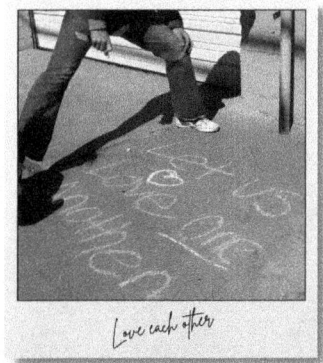

Love each other

After sixteen years of waiting, I finally sat down to write this book, knowing that it needed to be committed to the page. As I contacted various people who were there during this time, memories began flooding in as God had brought to memory all the great things He had done in showing us a slice of Heaven.

Jesus' name be lifted up high!

.